GRIEF JOURNAL

Name_____
Phone_____
Emergency Contact _____
_____

Daily Monitoring

Date_____

Mood 1 2 3 4 5 6 7 8 9 10

Today I struggled with_____
_____
_____
_____
_____
_____
_____
_____
_____
_____

Today I remembered_____
_____
_____
_____
_____
_____
_____
_____
_____

Sometimes I wish/think about _____
_____
_____
_____
_____

My goals toward feeling better _____
_____
_____
_____
_____

Self care _____
_____
_____
_____
_____

Today I am grateful for _____
_____
_____
_____
_____
_____
_____
_____
_____
_____

Daily Monitoring

Date_____

Mood   1   2   3   4   5   6   7   8   9   10

Today I struggled with_____
_____
_____
_____
_____
_____
_____
_____
_____
_____

Today I remembered_____
_____
_____
_____
_____
_____
_____
_____

Sometimes I wish/think about_____
_____
_____
_____
_____

My goals toward feeling better_____
_____
_____
_____
_____

Self care_____
_____
_____
_____
_____

Today I am grateful for_____
_____
_____
_____
_____
_____
_____
_____
_____
_____

Daily Monitoring

Date_____

Mood 1 2 3 4 5 6 7 8 9 10

Today I struggled with_____
_____
_____
_____
_____
_____
_____
_____
_____
_____

Today I remembered_____
_____
_____
_____
_____
_____
_____
_____
_____
_____

Sometimes I wish/think about _____
_____
_____
_____
_____

My goals toward feeling better _____
_____
_____
_____
_____

Self care _____
_____
_____
_____
_____

Today I am grateful for _____
_____
_____
_____
_____
_____
_____
_____
_____

Daily Monitoring

Date_____

Mood   1   2   3   4   5   6   7   8   9   10

Today I struggled with_____
_____
_____
_____
_____
_____
_____
_____
_____
_____
_____

Today I remembered_____
_____
_____
_____
_____
_____
_____
_____
_____

Sometimes I wish/think about _____
_____
_____
_____

My goals toward feeling better _____
_____
_____
_____

Self care _____
_____
_____
_____

Today I am grateful for _____
_____
_____
_____
_____
_____
_____
_____
_____

Daily Monitoring

Date_____

Mood   1   2   3   4   5   6   7   8   9   10

Today I struggled with_____
_____
_____
_____
_____
_____
_____
_____
_____
_____
_____

Today I remembered_____
_____
_____
_____
_____
_____
_____
_____
_____
_____

Sometimes I wish/think about _____
_____
_____
_____
_____

My goals toward feeling better _____
_____
_____
_____
_____

Self care _____
_____
_____
_____
_____

Today I am grateful for _____
_____
_____
_____
_____
_____
_____
_____
_____

Daily Monitoring

Date_____

Mood 1 2 3 4 5 6 7 8 9 10

Today I struggled with_____
_____
_____
_____
_____
_____
_____
_____
_____
_____

Today I remembered_____
_____
_____
_____
_____
_____
_____
_____
_____
_____

Sometimes I wish/think about _____
_____
_____
_____
_____

My goals toward feeling better _____
_____
_____
_____
_____

Self care _____
_____
_____
_____
_____

Today I am grateful for _____
_____
_____
_____
_____
_____
_____
_____
_____

Daily Monitoring

Date_____

Mood   1   2   3   4   5   6   7   8   9   10

Today I struggled with_____
_____
_____
_____
_____
_____
_____
_____
_____
_____

Today I remembered_____
_____
_____
_____
_____
_____
_____
_____
_____

Sometimes I wish/think about _____

_____

_____

_____

My goals toward feeling better _____

_____

_____

_____

Self care _____

_____

_____

_____

Today I am grateful for _____

_____

_____

_____

_____

_____

_____

_____

Daily Monitoring

Date_____

Mood 1 2 3 4 5 6 7 8 9 10

Today I struggled with_____
_____
_____
_____
_____
_____
_____
_____
_____

Today I remembered_____
_____
_____
_____
_____
_____
_____
_____
_____

Sometimes I wish/think about _____

_____
_____
_____

My goals toward feeling better _____

_____
_____
_____

Self care _____

_____
_____
_____

Today I am grateful for _____

_____
_____
_____
_____
_____
_____
_____
_____

Daily Monitoring

Date_____

Mood   1   2   3   4   5   6   7   8   9   10

Today I struggled with_____

_____
_____
_____
_____
_____
_____
_____
_____
_____

Today I remembered_____

_____
_____
_____
_____
_____
_____
_____
_____

Sometimes I wish/think about _____

_____

_____

_____

_____

My goals toward feeling better _____

_____

_____

_____

_____

Self care _____

_____

_____

_____

_____

Today I am grateful for _____

_____

_____

_____

_____

_____

_____

_____

_____

Daily Monitoring

Date_____

Mood   1   2   3   4   5   6   7   8   9   10

Today I struggled with_____
_____
_____
_____
_____
_____
_____
_____
_____
_____

Today I remembered_____
_____
_____
_____
_____
_____
_____
_____
_____

Sometimes I wish/think about _____

_____
_____
_____
_____

My goals toward feeling better _____

_____
_____
_____
_____

Self care _____

_____
_____
_____
_____

Today I am grateful for _____

_____
_____
_____
_____
_____
_____
_____

Daily Monitoring

Date_____

Mood 1 2 3 4 5 6 7 8 9 10

Today I struggled with_____
_____
_____
_____
_____
_____
_____
_____
_____
_____

Today I remembered_____
_____
_____
_____
_____
_____
_____
_____
_____

Sometimes I wish/think about _____

_____
_____
_____

My goals toward feeling better _____

_____
_____
_____

Self care _____

_____
_____
_____

Today I am grateful for _____

_____
_____
_____
_____
_____
_____
_____
_____

Daily Monitoring

Date_____

Mood 1 2 3 4 5 6 7 8 9 10

Today I struggled with_____

_____
_____
_____
_____
_____
_____
_____
_____
_____
_____

Today I remembered_____

_____
_____
_____
_____
_____
_____
_____
_____

Sometimes I wish/think about _____

_____
_____
_____
_____

My goals toward feeling better _____

_____
_____
_____
_____

Self care _____

_____
_____
_____
_____

Today I am grateful for _____

_____
_____
_____
_____
_____
_____
_____
_____
_____

Daily Monitoring

Date_____

Mood   1   2   3   4   5   6   7   8   9   10

Today I struggled with_____
_____
_____
_____
_____
_____
_____
_____
_____
_____

Today I remembered_____
_____
_____
_____
_____
_____
_____
_____
_____

Sometimes I wish/think about _____

_____
_____
_____
_____

My goals toward feeling better _____

_____
_____
_____
_____

Self care _____

_____
_____
_____
_____

Today I am grateful for _____

_____
_____
_____
_____
_____
_____
_____
_____
_____

Daily Monitoring

Date_____

Mood   1   2   3   4   5   6   7   8   9   10

Today I struggled with_____

_____
_____
_____
_____
_____
_____
_____
_____
_____

Today I remembered_____

_____
_____
_____
_____
_____
_____
_____
_____

Sometimes I wish/think about _____
_____
_____
_____
_____

My goals toward feeling better _____
_____
_____
_____
_____

Self care _____
_____
_____
_____
_____

Today I am grateful for _____
_____
_____
_____
_____
_____
_____
_____
_____
_____

Daily Monitoring

Date_____

Mood   1   2   3   4   5   6   7   8   9   10

Today I struggled with_____
_____
_____
_____
_____
_____
_____
_____
_____
_____

Today I remembered_____
_____
_____
_____
_____
_____
_____
_____
_____

Sometimes I wish/think about _____
_____
_____
_____
_____

My goals toward feeling better _____
_____
_____
_____
_____

Self care _____
_____
_____
_____
_____

Today I am grateful for _____
_____
_____
_____
_____
_____
_____
_____
_____

Daily Monitoring

Date_____

Mood   1   2   3   4   5   6   7   8   9   10

Today I struggled with_____
_____
_____
_____
_____
_____
_____
_____
_____
_____

Today I remembered_____
_____
_____
_____
_____
_____
_____
_____
_____

Sometimes I wish/think about _____
_____
_____
_____
_____

My goals toward feeling better _____
_____
_____
_____
_____

Self care _____
_____
_____
_____
_____

Today I am grateful for _____
_____
_____
_____
_____
_____
_____
_____
_____

Daily Monitoring

Date_____

Mood 1 2 3 4 5 6 7 8 9 10

Today I struggled with_____

_____
_____
_____
_____
_____
_____
_____
_____
_____

Today I remembered_____

_____
_____
_____
_____
_____
_____
_____
_____
_____

Sometimes I wish/think about _____
_____
_____
_____

My goals toward feeling better _____
_____
_____
_____

Self care _____
_____
_____
_____

Today I am grateful for _____
_____
_____
_____
_____
_____
_____
_____
_____

Daily Monitoring

Date_____

Mood 1 2 3 4 5 6 7 8 9 10

Today I struggled with_____

_____
_____
_____
_____
_____
_____
_____
_____
_____

Today I remembered_____

_____
_____
_____
_____
_____
_____
_____
_____

Sometimes I wish/think about_____
_____
_____
_____
_____

My goals toward feeling better_____
_____
_____
_____
_____

Self care_____
_____
_____
_____
_____

Today I am grateful for_____
_____
_____
_____
_____
_____
_____
_____
_____
_____

Daily Monitoring

Date_____

Mood   1   2   3   4   5   6   7   8   9   10

Today I struggled with_____
_____
_____
_____
_____
_____
_____
_____
_____
_____

Today I remembered_____
_____
_____
_____
_____
_____
_____
_____
_____

Sometimes I wish/think about _____

_____
_____
_____
_____

My goals toward feeling better _____

_____
_____
_____
_____

Self care _____

_____
_____
_____
_____

Today I am grateful for _____

_____
_____
_____
_____
_____
_____
_____
_____

Daily Monitoring

Date_____

Mood   1   2   3   4   5   6   7   8   9   10

Today I struggled with_____

_____
_____
_____
_____
_____
_____
_____
_____
_____

Today I remembered_____

_____
_____
_____
_____
_____
_____
_____
_____

Sometimes I wish/think about _____
_____
_____
_____
_____

My goals toward feeling better _____
_____
_____
_____
_____

Self care _____
_____
_____
_____
_____

Today I am grateful for _____
_____
_____
_____
_____
_____
_____
_____
_____
_____

Daily Monitoring

Date_____

Mood   1   2   3   4   5   6   7   8   9   10

Today I struggled with_____

_____
_____
_____
_____
_____
_____
_____
_____
_____

Today I remembered_____

_____
_____
_____
_____
_____
_____
_____
_____

Sometimes I wish/think about _____

_____

_____

_____

_____

My goals toward feeling better _____

_____

_____

_____

_____

Self care _____

_____

_____

_____

_____

Today I am grateful for _____

_____

_____

_____

_____

_____

_____

_____

_____

_____

Daily Monitoring

Date_____

Mood   1   2   3   4   5   6   7   8   9   10

Today I struggled with_____

_____
_____
_____
_____
_____
_____
_____
_____
_____
_____

Today I remembered_____

_____
_____
_____
_____
_____
_____
_____
_____

Sometimes I wish/think about _____

_____
_____
_____

My goals toward feeling better _____

_____
_____
_____

Self care _____

_____
_____
_____

Today I am grateful for _____

_____
_____
_____
_____
_____
_____
_____
_____

Daily Monitoring

Date_____

Mood   1   2   3   4   5   6   7   8   9   10

Today I struggled with_____
_____
_____
_____
_____
_____
_____
_____
_____
_____

Today I remembered_____
_____
_____
_____
_____
_____
_____
_____
_____
_____

Sometimes I wish/think about _____

_____
_____
_____
_____

My goals toward feeling better _____

_____
_____
_____
_____

Self care _____

_____
_____
_____
_____

Today I am grateful for _____

_____
_____
_____
_____
_____
_____
_____
_____
_____

Daily Monitoring

Date_____

Mood   1   2   3   4   5   6   7   8   9   10

Today I struggled with_____
_____
_____
_____
_____
_____
_____
_____
_____

Today I remembered_____
_____
_____
_____
_____
_____
_____
_____
_____

Sometimes I wish/think about _____
_____
_____
_____

My goals toward feeling better _____
_____
_____
_____

Self care _____
_____
_____
_____

Today I am grateful for _____
_____
_____
_____
_____
_____
_____
_____
_____

Daily Monitoring

Date_____

Mood 1 2 3 4 5 6 7 8 9 10

Today I struggled with_____
_____
_____
_____
_____
_____
_____
_____
_____
_____
_____

Today I remembered_____
_____
_____
_____
_____
_____
_____
_____
_____

Sometimes I wish/think about _____

_____

_____

_____

My goals toward feeling better _____

_____

_____

_____

Self care _____

_____

_____

_____

Today I am grateful for _____

_____

_____

_____

_____

_____

_____

_____

_____

Daily Monitoring

Date_____

Mood   1   2   3   4   5   6   7   8   9   10

Today I struggled with_____
_____
_____
_____
_____
_____
_____
_____
_____
_____

Today I remembered_____
_____
_____
_____
_____
_____
_____
_____
_____

Sometimes I wish/think about _____
_____
_____
_____

My goals toward feeling better _____
_____
_____
_____

Self care _____
_____
_____
_____

Today I am grateful for _____
_____
_____
_____
_____
_____
_____
_____
_____

Daily Monitoring

Date _____

Mood   1   2   3   4   5   6   7   8   9   10

Today I struggled with _____

_____
_____
_____
_____
_____
_____
_____
_____

Today I remembered _____

_____
_____
_____
_____
_____
_____
_____
_____

Sometimes I wish/think about _____
_____
_____
_____
_____

My goals toward feeling better _____
_____
_____
_____
_____

Self care _____
_____
_____
_____
_____

Today I am grateful for _____
_____
_____
_____
_____
_____
_____
_____
_____
_____

Daily Monitoring

Date_____

Mood 1 2 3 4 5 6 7 8 9 10

Today I struggled with_____
_____
_____
_____
_____
_____
_____
_____
_____
_____

Today I remembered_____
_____
_____
_____
_____
_____
_____
_____
_____

Sometimes I wish/think about _____

_____
_____
_____

My goals toward feeling better _____

_____
_____
_____

Self care _____

_____
_____
_____

Today I am grateful for _____

_____
_____
_____
_____
_____
_____
_____

Daily Monitoring

Date_____

Mood   1   2   3   4   5   6   7   8   9   10

Today I struggled with_____

_____
_____
_____
_____
_____
_____
_____
_____
_____

Today I remembered_____

_____
_____
_____
_____
_____
_____
_____
_____

Sometimes I wish/think about _____
_____
_____
_____
_____

My goals toward feeling better _____
_____
_____
_____
_____

Self care _____
_____
_____
_____
_____

Today I am grateful for _____
_____
_____
_____
_____
_____
_____
_____
_____
_____

Daily Monitoring

Date_____

Mood   1   2   3   4   5   6   7   8   9   10

Today I struggled with_____
_____
_____
_____
_____
_____
_____
_____
_____
_____

Today I remembered_____
_____
_____
_____
_____
_____
_____
_____
_____
_____

Sometimes I wish/think about _____
_____
_____
_____
_____

My goals toward feeling better _____
_____
_____
_____
_____

Self care _____
_____
_____
_____
_____

Today I am grateful for _____
_____
_____
_____
_____
_____
_____
_____
_____

Daily Monitoring

Date_____

Mood 1 2 3 4 5 6 7 8 9 10

Today I struggled with_____
_____
_____
_____
_____
_____
_____
_____
_____
_____

Today I remembered_____
_____
_____
_____
_____
_____
_____
_____
_____

Sometimes I wish/think about _____

_____

_____

_____

_____

My goals toward feeling better _____

_____

_____

_____

_____

Self care _____

_____

_____

_____

_____

Today I am grateful for _____

_____

_____

_____

_____

_____

_____

_____

_____

_____

Daily Monitoring

Date_____

Mood   1   2   3   4   5   6   7   8   9   10

Today I struggled with_____
_____
_____
_____
_____
_____
_____
_____
_____
_____

Today I remembered_____
_____
_____
_____
_____
_____
_____
_____
_____
_____

Sometimes I wish/think about _____

_____
_____
_____
_____

My goals toward feeling better _____

_____
_____
_____
_____

Self care _____

_____
_____
_____
_____

Today I am grateful for _____

_____
_____
_____
_____
_____
_____
_____
_____
_____
_____

Daily Monitoring

Date_____

Mood   1   2   3   4   5   6   7   8   9   10

Today I struggled with_____

_____
_____
_____
_____
_____
_____
_____
_____
_____

Today I remembered_____

_____
_____
_____
_____
_____
_____
_____

Sometimes I wish/think about _____
_____
_____
_____
_____

My goals toward feeling better _____
_____
_____
_____
_____

Self care _____
_____
_____
_____
_____

Today I am grateful for _____
_____
_____
_____
_____
_____
_____
_____
_____
_____

Daily Monitoring

Date_____

Mood 1 2 3 4 5 6 7 8 9 10

Today I struggled with_____
_____
_____
_____
_____
_____
_____
_____
_____
_____

Today I remembered_____
_____
_____
_____
_____
_____
_____
_____
_____
_____

Sometimes I wish/think about _____

_____
_____
_____

My goals toward feeling better _____

_____
_____
_____

Self care _____

_____
_____
_____

Today I am grateful for _____

_____
_____
_____
_____
_____
_____
_____

Daily Monitoring

Date_____

Mood   1   2   3   4   5   6   7   8   9   10

Today I struggled with_____

_____
_____
_____
_____
_____
_____
_____
_____

Today I remembered_____

_____
_____
_____
_____
_____
_____
_____
_____

Sometimes I wish/think about_____
_____
_____
_____

My goals toward feeling better_____
_____
_____
_____

Self care_____
_____
_____
_____

Today I am grateful for_____
_____
_____
_____
_____
_____
_____
_____
_____

Daily Monitoring

Date_____

Mood   1   2   3   4   5   6   7   8   9   10

Today I struggled with_____

_____
_____
_____
_____
_____
_____
_____
_____
_____

Today I remembered_____

_____
_____
_____
_____
_____
_____
_____
_____

Sometimes I wish/think about _____
_____
_____
_____
_____

My goals toward feeling better _____
_____
_____
_____
_____

Self care _____
_____
_____
_____
_____

Today I am grateful for _____
_____
_____
_____
_____
_____
_____
_____
_____

Daily Monitoring

Date_____

Mood   1   2   3   4   5   6   7   8   9   10

Today I struggled with_____

_____
_____
_____
_____
_____
_____
_____
_____
_____
_____

Today I remembered_____

_____
_____
_____
_____
_____
_____
_____
_____

Sometimes I wish/think about _____
_____
_____
_____
_____

My goals toward feeling better _____
_____
_____
_____
_____

Self care _____
_____
_____
_____
_____

Today I am grateful for _____
_____
_____
_____
_____
_____
_____
_____
_____

Daily Monitoring

Date_____

Mood 1 2 3 4 5 6 7 8 9 10

Today I struggled with_____

_____
_____
_____
_____
_____
_____
_____
_____
_____

Today I remembered_____

_____
_____
_____
_____
_____
_____
_____
_____

Sometimes I wish/think about _____

_____
_____
_____

My goals toward feeling better _____

_____
_____
_____

Self care _____

_____
_____
_____

Today I am grateful for _____

_____
_____
_____
_____
_____
_____
_____
_____

Daily Monitoring

Date_____

Mood   1   2   3   4   5   6   7   8   9   10

Today I struggled with_____
_____
_____
_____
_____
_____
_____
_____
_____
_____

Today I remembered_____
_____
_____
_____
_____
_____
_____
_____
_____

Sometimes I wish/think about_____

_____
_____
_____
_____

My goals toward feeling better_____

_____
_____
_____
_____

Self care_____

_____
_____
_____
_____

Today I am grateful for_____

_____
_____
_____
_____
_____
_____
_____
_____
_____

Daily Monitoring

Date_____

Mood   1   2   3   4   5   6   7   8   9   10

Today I struggled with_____
_____
_____
_____
_____
_____
_____
_____
_____
_____
_____

Today I remembered_____
_____
_____
_____
_____
_____
_____
_____
_____

Sometimes I wish/think about _____

_____
_____
_____

My goals toward feeling better _____

_____
_____
_____

Self care _____

_____
_____
_____

Today I am grateful for _____

_____
_____
_____
_____
_____
_____
_____

Daily Monitoring

Date_____

Mood   1   2   3   4   5   6   7   8   9   10

Today I struggled with_____

_____
_____
_____
_____
_____
_____
_____
_____
_____

Today I remembered_____

_____
_____
_____
_____
_____
_____
_____
_____

Sometimes I wish/think about _____
_____
_____
_____

My goals toward feeling better _____
_____
_____
_____

Self care _____
_____
_____
_____

Today I am grateful for _____
_____
_____
_____
_____
_____
_____
_____
_____

Daily Monitoring

Date_____

Mood   1   2   3   4   5   6   7   8   9   10

Today I struggled with_____
_____
_____
_____
_____
_____
_____
_____
_____
_____

Today I remembered_____
_____
_____
_____
_____
_____
_____
_____
_____
_____

Sometimes I wish/think about _____

_____
_____
_____
_____

My goals toward feeling better _____

_____
_____
_____
_____

Self care _____

_____
_____
_____
_____

Today I am grateful for _____

_____
_____
_____
_____
_____
_____
_____
_____
_____

Daily Monitoring

Date _____

Mood   1   2   3   4   5   6   7   8   9   10

Today I struggled with _____
_____
_____
_____
_____
_____
_____
_____
_____
_____

Today I remembered _____
_____
_____
_____
_____
_____
_____
_____
_____

Sometimes I wish/think about _____

_____
_____
_____

My goals toward feeling better _____

_____
_____
_____

Self care _____

_____
_____
_____

Today I am grateful for _____

_____
_____
_____
_____
_____
_____
_____
_____

Daily Monitoring

Date_____

Mood   1   2   3   4   5   6   7   8   9   10

Today I struggled with_____
_____
_____
_____
_____
_____
_____
_____
_____
_____

Today I remembered_____
_____
_____
_____
_____
_____
_____
_____
_____
_____

Sometimes I wish/think about _____
_____
_____
_____

My goals toward feeling better _____
_____
_____
_____

Self care _____
_____
_____
_____

Today I am grateful for _____
_____
_____
_____
_____
_____
_____
_____
_____

Daily Monitoring

Date_____

Mood   1   2   3   4   5   6   7   8   9   10

Today I struggled with_____
_____
_____
_____
_____
_____
_____
_____
_____

Today I remembered_____
_____
_____
_____
_____
_____
_____
_____
_____

Sometimes I wish/think about _____

_____
_____
_____

My goals toward feeling better _____

_____
_____
_____

Self care _____

_____
_____
_____

Today I am grateful for _____

_____
_____
_____
_____
_____
_____
_____

Daily Monitoring

Date_____

Mood   1   2   3   4   5   6   7   8   9   10

Today I struggled with_____

_____

_____

_____

_____

_____

_____

_____

_____

_____

Today I remembered_____

_____

_____

_____

_____

_____

_____

_____

Sometimes I wish/think about _____

_____
_____
_____

My goals toward feeling better _____

_____
_____
_____

Self care _____

_____
_____
_____

Today I am grateful for _____

_____
_____
_____
_____
_____
_____
_____

Daily Monitoring

Date_____

Mood   1   2   3   4   5   6   7   8   9   10

Today I struggled with_____
_____
_____
_____
_____
_____
_____
_____
_____
_____
_____

Today I remembered_____
_____
_____
_____
_____
_____
_____
_____
_____
_____

Sometimes I wish/think about _____
_____
_____
_____

My goals toward feeling better _____
_____
_____
_____

Self care _____
_____
_____
_____

Today I am grateful for _____
_____
_____
_____
_____
_____
_____
_____
_____

Daily Monitoring

Date_____

Mood   1   2   3   4   5   6   7   8   9   10

Today I struggled with_____
_____
_____
_____
_____
_____
_____
_____
_____
_____
_____

Today I remembered_____
_____
_____
_____
_____
_____
_____
_____
_____

Sometimes I wish/think about _____

_____

_____

_____

_____

My goals toward feeling better _____

_____

_____

_____

_____

Self care _____

_____

_____

_____

_____

Today I am grateful for _____

_____

_____

_____

_____

_____

_____

_____

_____

_____

Daily Monitoring

Date_____

Mood 1 2 3 4 5 6 7 8 9 10

Today I struggled with_____

_____
_____
_____
_____
_____
_____
_____
_____
_____

Today I remembered_____

_____
_____
_____
_____
_____
_____
_____
_____

Sometimes I wish/think about _____
_____
_____
_____
_____

My goals toward feeling better _____
_____
_____
_____
_____

Self care _____
_____
_____
_____
_____

Today I am grateful for _____
_____
_____
_____
_____
_____
_____
_____
_____
_____

Printed in Great Britain
by Amazon